M0000002762

DEVOTIONS
FOR
ENCOURAGEMENT
&MATURITY

2 CORINTHIANS & JAMES

DEVOTIONS
FOR
ENCOURAGEMENT
&MATURITY

2 CORINTHIANS & JAMES

Warren W. Wiersbe

HONOR **HB** BOOKS

Inspiration and Motivation for the Seasons of Life

COOK COMMUNICATIONS MINISTRIES
Colorado Springs, Colorado • Paris, Ontario
KINGSWAY COMMUNICATIONS LTD
Eastbourne, England

Honor® is an imprint of
Cook Communications Ministries, Colorado Springs, CO 80918
Cook Communications, Paris, Ontario
Kingsway Communications, Eastbourne, England

DEVOTIONS FOR ENCOURAGEMENT AND MATURITY
© 2005 by Warren Wiersbe

All rights reserved. No part of this book may be reproduced without written permission, except for brief quotations in books and critical reviews. For information, write Cook Communications Ministries, 4050 Lee Vance View, Colorado Springs, CO 80918.

Cover Design: Jackson Design CO, LLC/Greg Jackson

First Printing, 2005
Printed in the United States of America

Printing/Year
1 2 3 4 5 6 7 8 9 10   /   10 09 08 07 06 05

Unless otherwise noted, Scripture quotations are taken from the HOLY BIBLE, NEW INTERNATIONAL VERSION®. Copyright © 1973, 1978, 1984 by International Bible Society. Used by permission of Zondervan. All rights reserved. Scripture quotations marked KJV are taken from the King James Version of the Bible. Public Domain. Italics in Scripture have been added by the author for emphasis.

This book was originally published as two paperback editions in 1994 and 1995, compiled by Stan Campbell. Each devotional reading is adapted from Warren Wiersbe's "Be" series.

ISBN 1-56292-699-3

Encouragement

Thirty Daily Readings from the Book of 2 Corinthians

W hy?"
        That's the easiest question to ask and the hardest to answer. Why do people suffer? Why do our best-laid plans fall apart? Why do the people we love make life difficult for us? Why doesn't God answer our prayers and change our circumstances? Why can't life be easier?

Why, Lord? And why *me*?

We live in difficult days, and they aren't about to get easier. Each stage of life brings with it special joys and challenges, and also special trials and sorrows. Nobody is exempt from the battles of life.

Though he lived centuries ago, the apostle Paul knew a great deal about the problems and the difficulties people go through today. Human nature and human problems haven't really changed that much since Paul wrote the letter we call 2 Corinthians. His theme? "Be encouraged! It's always too soon to quit!"

This is the most intimate letter Paul ever wrote. In it, he bared his heart and described some of the difficult experiences he went through and how the Lord gave him the encouragement he needed day after day. Paul didn't just *endure* the trials of life, nor did he selfishly try to *escape* them. Instead, he learned how to *enlist* them to build a life that triumphed over pain and problems and brought glory to God.

Your daily study of this ancient letter can help you follow Paul's example and trust Paul's God, the God who still says, "My grace is sufficient for you" (2 Cor. 12:9). Paul can show you how to make your difficulties work *for* you and not *against* you.

Our English word "discourage" means "without heart." When Christ is Lord of your life, He can put into your heart the courage you need to face life with its problems and be a victor, not a victim.

No matter what the feelings within you or the circumstances around you or the pressures against you, *you can be encouraged!* And you can encourage others.

Day 1

God Is in Control

Read 2 Corinthians 1:1–5

> *"Praise be to the God and Father of our Lord Jesus Christ,*
> *the Father of compassion and the God of all comfort, who comforts*
> *us in all our troubles, so that we can comfort those in any trouble*
> *with the comfort we ourselves have received from God."*

2 CORINTHIANS 1:3–4

Paul began his letter with a doxology. He certainly could not sing about his circumstances, but he could sing about the God who is in control of all circumstances. Paul had learned that praise is an important factor in achieving victory over discouragement and depression.

In 2 Corinthians Paul praised God for *present* blessings, for what God was accomplishing then and there. During the horrors of the Thirty Years' War, Pastor Martin Rinkart faithfully served the people in Eilenburg, Saxony. He conducted as many as forty funerals a day, a total of more than four thousand during his ministry. Yet out of this devastating experience, he wrote a "table grace" for his children, which today we use as a hymn of thanksgiving:

> Now thank we all our God,
> With heart and hands and voices,
> Who wondrous things hath done,
> In whom His world rejoices!

Whatever the Father did for Jesus when He was ministering on earth, He is able to do for us today. We are dear to the Father because

His Son is dear to Him, and we are citizens of "the kingdom of the Son he loves" (Col. 1:13). We are precious to the Father, and He will see to it that the pressures of life do not destroy us.

Applying God's Truth:

1. As you begin this book, what reasons do you have to offer God thanksgiving and praise?

2. For what are you seeking comfort today?

3. What might you need to do to better comprehend the love that God has for you?

Day 2

Leading the Way

Read 2 Corinthians 1:6–7

"Our hope for you is firm, because we know that just as you share in our sufferings, so also you share in our comfort."

2 CORINTHIANS 1:7

One of my favorite preachers was Dr. George W. Truett, who pastored First Baptist Church of Dallas, Texas, for nearly fifty years. In one of his sermons, he told about an unbelieving couple whose baby died suddenly. Dr. Truett conducted the funeral and later had the joy of seeing both parents trust Jesus Christ.

Many months later, a young mother lost her baby, and Dr. Truett was called to bring her comfort. Nothing he shared with her seemed to help her. But at the funeral service, the newly converted mother stepped to the young woman's side and said, "I passed through this, and I know what you are passing through. God called me, and through the darkness I came to Him. He has comforted me, and He will comfort you!"

Later Dr. Truett said, "The first mother did more for the second mother than I could have done, maybe in days and months; for the first young mother had traveled the road of suffering herself."

We do not need to experience exactly the same trials as others in order to be able to share God's encouragement. If we have experienced God's comfort, then "we can comfort those in any trouble" (v. 4). Of course, if we have experienced similar tribulations, they can help us identify better with others and know better how they feel; but

our experiences cannot alter the comfort of God. That remains sufficient and efficient no matter what our own experiences may have
been.

Applying God's Truth:

1. Can you recall a similar instance in your life or the life of a
friend or family member that caused you to question God's love or
doubt His power? How did you deal with your feelings?

2. Which do you tend to share with others more frequently: your
sufferings, or a sense of comfort? Why?

3. Does your faith in God tend to change based on the amount of
comfort you feel? Explain.

Day 3

Special Sufferings

Read 2 Corinthians 1:8–24

*"In our hearts we felt the sentence of death. But this happened that
we might not rely on ourselves but on God, who raises the dead."*

2 CORINTHIANS 1:9

God permits trials to come. In the Greek language, there are ten basic words for suffering, and Paul used five of them in this letter. There are some sufferings that we endure simply because we are human and subject to pain; but there are other sufferings that come because we are God's people and want to serve Him.

We must never think that trouble is an accident. For us believers, everything is a divine appointment. God encourages us in all our tribulations by teaching us from His Word that it is He who permits trials to come. He encourages us further by reminding us that *He is in control of trials* (see v. 9). Paul was weighed down like a beast of burden with a load too heavy to bear. But God knew just how much Paul could take, and He kept the situation under control.

We do not know what the specific "trouble" was, but it was great enough to make Paul think he was going to die. Whether it was peril from his many enemies, serious illness, or special satanic attack, we do not know; but we do know that God controlled the circumstances and protected His servant. Paul may have despaired of life, but God did not despair of Paul.

Applying God's Truth:

1. How do you feel toward God when you encounter suffering?

2. Can you think of past personal trials which, looking back, you can see why God permitted them to happen?

3. What are some of your most pressing current trials? What can you do to ensure that you remain focused on God during these trying times?

Day 4

Religion Gone Wrong

Read 2 Corinthians 2:1–11

> *"If you forgive anyone, I also forgive him. And what I have
> forgiven—if there was anything to forgive—I have forgiven in the sight
> of Christ for your sake, in order that Satan might not outwit us."*
>
> 2 CORINTHIANS 2:10–11

I have often quoted an anonymous rhyme that perfectly describes one of the most frequent problems we have as the people of God:

> To live above with saints we love,
> Will certainly be glory!
> To live below with saints we know,
> Well, that's another story!

One of the members of the Corinthian church caused Paul a great deal of pain. We are not sure if this is the same man Paul wrote about in 1 Corinthians 5, the man who was living in open fornication, or if it was another person, someone who publicly challenged Paul's apostolic authority. Paul had made a quick visit to Corinth to deal with this problem (see 12:14; 13:1) and had also written a painful letter to the church about the situation. In all of this, he revealed a compassionate heart.

Paul could have exercised his apostolic authority and commanded the people to respect him and obey him, but he preferred to minister with patience and love. Love always considers the feelings of others and seeks to put their good ahead of everything else.

When I was a child, I didn't always appreciate the punishment that my parents gave me. But now that I look back, I can thank God that they loved me enough to discipline me. Now I understand what they really meant when they said, "This hurts us more than it hurts you."

Applying God's Truth:

1. When people offend you, are you quick to "reveal a compassionate heart"? If not, what is your usual course of action?

2. On a scale of 1 (least) to 10 (most), how much of each of the following qualities do you normally exhibit in a conflict situation: Love? Patience? Logic? Force? Empathy?

3. How do you think Satan tends to work through our personal conflicts?

Day 5

Join the Parade

Read 2 Corinthians 2:12–17

"Thanks be to God, who always leads us in triumphal procession in Christ and through us spreads everywhere the fragrance of the knowledge of him."

2 Corinthians 2:14

Paul was sure that *God was leading him in triumph.* The picture here is that of the "Roman triumph," the special tribute that Rome gave to its conquering generals. If a commander in chief won a complete victory over the enemy on foreign soil, and if he killed at least five thousand enemy soldiers and gained new territory for the emperor, then that commander in chief was entitled to a Roman triumph. The processional would include the commander riding in a golden chariot, surrounded by his officers. The parade would also include a display of the spoils of battle, as well as the captive enemy soldiers. The Roman priests would also be in the parade, carrying burning incense to pay tribute to the victorious army.

Jesus Christ, our great commander in chief, came to foreign soil (this earth) and completely defeated the enemy (Satan). Instead of killing five thousand persons, He gave life to more than five thousand persons—to three thousand plus at Pentecost and to another two thousand plus shortly after Pentecost (see Acts 2:41; 4:4). Jesus Christ claimed the spoils of battle—lost souls who had been in bondage to sin and Satan. What a splendid victory!

The sons of the victorious generals would walk behind their father's chariot, sharing in his victory; and that is where believers are today—following in Christ's triumph. We do not fight *for* victory; we fight *from* victory. Neither in Asia Minor nor in Corinth did the situation look like victory to Paul, but he believed God—and God turned defeat into victory.

Applying God's Truth:

1. List some victories and reasons you have to feel triumphant today.

2. Does it *feel* as if you are on the winner's side in your spiritual battle, or do you have to accept it by faith?

3. What battles are you fighting on your own? How do you need God's help?

Day 6

Written on the Heart

Read 2 Corinthians 3:1–6

"You show that you are a letter from Christ, the result of our ministry,
written not with ink but with the Spirit of the living God,
not on tablets of stone but on tablets of human hearts."

2 CORINTHIANS 3:3

When God gave the law, He wrote it on tables of stone, and those tables were placed in the ark of the covenant. Even though the Israelites could read the two tables, this experience did not change their lives. The law is an external thing, and people need an *internal* power if their lives are to be transformed. Legalists can admonish us with "Do this!" or "Don't do that!" But they cannot give us the power to obey. If we do obey, often it is not from the heart—and we end up worse than we were before!

The ministry of grace changes the heart. The Spirit of God takes the Word of God and writes it on the heart. The Corinthians were wicked sinners when Paul came to them, but his ministry of the gospel of God's grace completely changed their lives (see 1 Cor. 6:9–11). Their experience of God's grace certainly meant more to them than the letters of commendation carried by the false teachers. The Corinthian believers were lovingly written on Paul's heart, and the Spirit of God had written the truth on their hearts, making them "living epistles of Christ."

The test of ministry is changed lives, not press releases or statistics. It is much easier for legalists to boast, because they can "measure" their ministry by external standards. Believers who patiently minister by the Spirit of God must leave the results with the Lord. How tragic that the Corinthians followed the boastful Judaizers and broke the heart of the apostle who had rescued them from judgment.

Applying God's Truth:

1. Since you are a "letter from Christ," what would you say is the message that is written on the tablet of your human heart?

2. Can you think of any "external" religious rules you follow because of obligation rather than genuine gratitude or worship?

3. In what way(s) do you attempt to measure your ministry as a Christian?

Day 7

Glory: Past and Present

Read 2 Corinthians 3:7–11

"If what was fading away came with glory, how much
greater is the glory of that which lasts!"

2 CORINTHIANS 3:11

Paul wrote at a period in history when the ages were overlapping. The New Covenant of grace had come in, but the temple services were still being carried on, and the nation of Israel was still living under law. In AD 70, the city of Jerusalem and the temple would be destroyed by the Romans, and that would mark the end of the Jewish religious system.

The Judaizers wanted the Corinthian believers to go back under the law, to "mix" the two covenants. "Why go back to that which is temporary and fading away?" Paul asked. "Live in the glory of the New Covenant, which is getting greater and greater." The glory of the law is but the glory of past history, while the glory of the New Covenant is the glory of present experience.

The glory of the law was fading in Paul's day, and today that glory is found only in the records in the Bible. The nation of Israel has no temple or priesthood. If they did build a temple, there would be no *shekinah* glory dwelling in the Holy of Holies. The law of Moses is a religion with a most glorious past, but it has no glory today. The light is gone; all that remain are the shadows (see Col. 2:16–17).

But the ministry of grace is internal (see 2 Cor. 3:1–3); it brings life (see vv. 4–6), and it involves increasing glory (see vv. 7–11).

Applying God's Truth:

1. Do you know people who try to focus more on Old Testament law (rules and regulations) than on the New Covenant of grace? How do they do so?

2. What are some temporal things that people try to "glory" in?

3. In your own life, do you tend to dwell more on the "light" of past accomplishments than in the "glory" of the here and now? Explain.

Day 8

Law and Legalism

Read 2 Corinthians 3:12–18

"Now the Lord is the Spirit, and where the Spirit of the Lord is, there is freedom."
2 CORINTHIANS 3:17

The result of Old Covenant ministry is bondage; but the result of New Covenant ministry is freedom in the Spirit. Legalism keeps people immature, and immature people must live by rules and regulations (see Gal. 4:1–7). God wants His children to obey, not because of an external code (the law), but because of internal character (the Spirit). Christians do not live under the law, but this does not mean that we are lawless! The Spirit of God writes the Word of God on our hearts, and we obey our Father because of the new life He has given us within.

The lure of legalism is still with us. False cults prey on professed Christians and church members, as did the Judaizers in Paul's day. We must learn to recognize false cults and reject their teachings. But there are also gospel-preaching churches that have legalistic tendencies and keep their members immature, guilty, and afraid. They spend a great deal of time dealing with the externals, and they neglect the cultivation of the inner life. They exalt standards, and they denounce sin, but they fail to magnify the Lord Jesus Christ. Sad to say, some New Testament churches have an Old Testament ministry.

Paul said that his own ministry was triumphant (see 2 Cor. 2:14) and glorious (see 3:7–18). The two go together. When our ministry involves the glory of God—we cannot quit!

Applying God's Truth:

1. What are some evidences of "freedom in the Spirit" that you have observed in your life?

2. How do you prevent legalistic thinking from affecting your spiritual freedom?

3. How could your personal ministry become more triumphant? More glorious?

Day 9

Motivation for Ministry

Read 2 Corinthians 4:1–6

"Since through God's mercy we have this ministry, we do not lose heart."
2 CORINTHIANS 4:1

The way we look at our ministry helps to determine how we will ful-fill it. If we look on serving Christ as a burden instead of a privilege, we will be a drudge and do only what is required of us. Some people even look upon Christian service as a punishment from God. When Paul considered the fact that he was a minister of Jesus Christ, he was overwhelmed by the grace and mercy of God.

His positive attitude toward the ministry kept him from being a quitter. He confessed to the Corinthians that his trials in Asia Minor had almost brought him to despair (see 1:8). In spite of his great gifts and vast experience, Paul was human and subject to human frailties. But how could he lose heart when he was involved in such a wonderful ministry? Had God entrusted this ministry to him so that he would fail? Of course not! With the divine calling came the divine enabling; he knew that God would see him through.

A discouraged Methodist preacher wrote to the great Scottish preacher Alexander Whyte to ask his counsel. Should he leave the ministry? "Never think of giving up preaching!" Whyte wrote to him. "The angels around the throne envy you your great work!" That was the kind of reply Paul would have written, the kind of reply all of us need to ponder whenever we feel that our work is in vain.

Applying God's Truth:

1. Under what circumstance are you most prone to "give up" spiritually?

2. How would it help you to dwell on God's mercy during times when it becomes difficult to keep going?

3. On a scale of 1 to 10, where 1 = burden and 10 = privilege, where would you rate your feelings toward your personal ministry?

Day 10

Hidden Treasure

Read 2 Corinthians 4:7–18

> *"We have this treasure in jars of clay to show that this all-surpassing power is from God and not from us."*
>
> 2 CORINTHIANS 4:7

Sometimes God permits our vessels to be jarred so that some of the treasure will spill out and enrich others. Suffering reveals not only the weakness of man but also the glory of God. Paul presented a series of paradoxes in this paragraph: earthen vessels—power of God; the dying Jesus—the life of Jesus; death working—life working. The natural mind cannot understand this kind of spiritual truth and therefore cannot understand why Christians triumph over suffering.

Not only must we focus on the treasure and not on the vessel, but we must also focus on the Master and not on the servant. If we suffer, it is for Jesus' sake. If we die to self, it is so that the life of Christ may be revealed in us. If we go through trials, it is so that Christ may be glorified. And all of this is for the sake of others. As we serve Christ, death works in us—but life works in those to whom we minister.

Dr. John Henry Jowett said, "Ministry that costs nothing, accomplishes nothing." He was right. A pastor friend and I once heard a young man preach an eloquent sermon, but it lacked something. "There was something missing," I said to my friend, and he replied, "Yes, and it won't be there until his heart is broken. After he has suffered awhile, he will have a message worth listening to."

Applying God's Truth:

1. Think of yourself as a vessel that carries the treasure of God, and then try to describe yourself in such terms (large or small, strong or fragile, new or antique, etc.).

2. When was the last time you felt "jarred" significantly—to the point of almost breaking? How did you handle the situation?

3. When most people look at your life, what do you think they see: yourself, or the treasure you contain? Why?

Day 11

Mobile Homes

Read 2 Corinthians 5:1–10

"We are always confident and know that as long as we are at
home in the body we are away from the Lord."

2 Corinthians 5:6

The people of God can be found in one of two places: either in heaven or on earth (see Eph. 3:15). None of them is in the grave, in hell, or in any "intermediate place" between earth and heaven. Believers on earth are "at home in the body" (v. 6), while believers who have died are "absent from the body" (v. 8 KJV). Believers on earth are "absent from the Lord" (v. 6 KJV), while believers in heaven are "present with the Lord" (v. 8 KJV).

Because he had this knowledge and confidence, Paul was not afraid of suffering and trials, or even of dangers. He was willing to "lose his life" for the sake of Christ and the ministry of the gospel. He walked by faith and not by sight (see v. 7). He looked at the eternal unseen, not the temporal seen (see 4:18). Heaven was not simply a *destination* for Paul: It was a *motivation*. Like the heroes of faith in Hebrews 11, he looked for the heavenly city (see vv. 13–16) and governed his life by eternal values.

Paul had courage for the conflict and would not lose heart. He had a glorious ministry that transformed lives. He had a valuable treasure in the earthen vessel of his body, and he wanted to share that treasure with a bankrupt world. He had a confident faith that conquered fear, and he had a future hope that was both a destination and a motivation. No wonder Paul was more than a conqueror! (See Rom. 8:37.) Every believer in Jesus Christ has these same marvelous possessions and can find through them courage for the conflict.

Applying God's Truth:

1. To what extent would you say you are so confident of heaven that no problem on earth can significantly concern you?

2. How could heaven become more of a motivation for you, and not just a destination?

3. On a scale of 1 to 10, where 1 = living by sight and 10 = living by faith, where would you say you are right now?

Day 12

Dying to Live

Read 2 Corinthians 5:11–15

"He died for all, that those who live should no longer live for themselves but for him who died for them and was raised again."

2 CORINTHIANS 5:15

It has well been said, "Christ died our death for us that we might live His life for Him." If we, who were lost sinners, have been to the cross and been saved, how can we spend the rest of our lives in selfishness?

In 1858, Frances Ridley Havergal visited Germany with her father who was getting treatment for his afflicted eyes. While in a pastor's home, she saw a picture of the crucifixion of Jesus on the wall, with the words under it: "I did this for thee. What hast thou done for Me?" Quickly she took a piece of paper and wrote a poem based on that motto, but she was not satisfied with it, so she threw the paper into the fireplace. The paper came out unharmed! Later, her father encouraged her to publish the poem; and we sing it today to a tune composed by Philip P. Bliss.

I gave My life for thee,
My precious blood I shed,
That thou might'st ransomed be,
And quickened from the dead;
I gave, I gave My life for thee,
What hast thou giv'n for Me?

Christ died that we might live *through* Him and *for* Him, and that we might live *with* Him. Because of Calvary, believers are going to heaven to live with Christ forever!

Applying God's Truth:

1. Think back a year. Are you "living for Christ" more effectively today than you did then, less effectively, or about the same? Why?

2. Make a mental list of all the things Christ has done for you—both generally and specifically.

3. List the ways you are living for yourself and compare that list to the ways you are living for Christ. Where do your primary interests lie?

Day 13

Representing the King

Read 2 Corinthians 5:16–21

> *"We are therefore Christ's ambassadors, as though God were making his appeal through us. We implore you on Christ's behalf: Be reconciled to God."*

2 CORINTHIANS 5:20

Since Christians in this world are the ambassadors of Christ, this means that the world is in rebellion against God. He has sent His ambassadors into the world to declare peace, not war. We represent Jesus Christ (see 4:5; John 20:21). If sinners reject us and our message, it is Jesus Christ who is actually rejected (see Luke 10:16). What a great privilege it is to be heaven's ambassadors to the rebellious sinners of this world!

When I was a young pastor, it used to embarrass me somewhat to make visits and confront people with the claims of Christ. Then it came to me that I was a privileged person, an ambassador of the King of kings! There was nothing to be embarrassed about. In fact, the people I visited should have been grateful that one of Christ's ambassadors came to see them.

God has not declared war on the world; at the cross He declared peace. But one day, He *will* declare war; and then it will be too late for those who have rejected the Savior (see 2 Thess. 1:3–10). Satan is seeking to tear everything apart in this world, but Christ and His church are involved in the ministry of reconciliation, bringing things back together, and back to God.

Ministry is not easy. If we are to succeed, we must be motivated by the fear of the Lord, the love of Christ, and the commission that He has given to us. What a privilege it is to serve Him!

Applying God's Truth:

1. Create what you think would be a good job description for an "ambassador of Christ."

2. What are some potential drawbacks of being an ambassador?

3. Who are some people to whom you could become an ambassador of Christ—people who might not hear the gospel from anyone else?

Day 14

An Attitude of Gratitude

Read 2 Corinthians 6

"We commend ourselves in every way: in great endurance; in troubles, hardships and distresses; in beatings, imprisonments and riots; in hard work, sleepless nights and hunger ... having nothing, and yet possessing everything."

2 CORINTHIANS 6:4–5, 10

What a price Paul paid to be faithful in his ministry! And yet how little the Corinthians really appreciated all he did for them. They brought sorrow to his heart, yet he was "always rejoicing" in Jesus Christ (v. 10). He became poor that they might become rich (see 1 Cor. 1:5; 2 Cor. 8:9). The Greek word translated "poor" means "the complete destitution of a beggar."

Was Paul wrong in appealing for their appreciation? I don't think so. Too many churches are prone to take for granted the sacrificial ministry of pastors, missionaries, and faithful church officers. Paul was not begging for praise, but he was reminding his friends in Corinth that his ministry to them had cost him dearly.

Of course, in all of this personal testimony, Paul was refuting the malicious accusations of the Judaizers. How much had *they* suffered for the people of Corinth? What price had *they* paid for their ministry? Like most cultists today, these false teachers stole someone else's converts; they did not seek to win the lost themselves.

It has well been said, "If you want to find gratitude, look in the dictionary." Are we showing gratitude to those who have ministered to us?

Applying God's Truth:

1. What are some sacrifices you have made for others lately that didn't seem to be appreciated? How did you feel?

2. How careful are you to show gratitude for the good things other people do for *you?*

3. Can you think of some negative personal experiences (sacrifices) you have faced that turned out to be very beneficial for other people?

Day 15

A Separate Peace

Read 2 Corinthians 7

"Since we have these promises, dear friends, let us purify
ourselves from everything that contaminates body and spirit,
perfecting holiness out of reverence for God."

2 CORINTHIANS 7:1

God blesses those who separate themselves from sin and cleave unto the Lord.

Because of God's gracious promises, we have some spiritual responsibilities. We must cleanse ourselves once and for all of anything that defiles us. It is not enough to ask God to cleanse us; we must clean up our own lives and get rid of those things that make it easy for us to sin. None of us can legislate for any other believer; each one of us knows the problems of our own heart and life.

Too often Christians deal with symptoms and not causes. We keep confessing the same sins because we have not gotten to the root of the trouble and "purified ourselves." Perhaps there is something that "contaminates" us—a filthiness of the flesh that feeds the old sinful nature (see Rom. 13:14). Or it may be filthiness of the spirit, an attitude that is sinful. The Prodigal Son was guilty of sins of the flesh, but his "moral" elder brother was guilty of sins of the spirit. He could not even get along with his own father (see Luke 15:11–32).

But cleansing ourselves is only half of the responsibility; we must also be "perfecting holiness out of reverence for God" (2 Cor. 7:1). This is a constant process as we grow in grace and knowledge (see 2 Peter 3:18).

Applying God's Truth:

1. Can you think of spiritual "symptoms" you frequently deal with that may suggest a deeper root problem?

2. What are some ways that you can consciously separate yourself from sinful things?

3. Do you work hard at remaining separate from sin, or do you just hope that God will remove your temptations some day?

Day 16

Grace Giving

Read 2 Corinthians 8:1–7

> *"We want you to know about the grace that God has given the*
> *Macedonian churches. Out of the most severe trial, their overflowing*
> *joy and their extreme poverty welled up in rich generosity."*
>
> 2 CORINTHIANS 8:1–2

When we have experienced the grace of God in our life, we will not use difficult circumstances as an excuse for not giving. In my first pastorate, we had a great need for a new church building, but some of the people opposed a building program because of the "economic situation." Apparently the steel mills were planning to go on strike, the refineries were going to shut down, and the railroads were having problems … and it seemed like a risky time to build. But there were enough people who believed in "grace giving" so that the church did erect a new sanctuary—in spite of the strikes, shutdowns, layoffs, and other economic problems. Grace giving means giving in spite of circumstances.

It is possible to give generously but not give enthusiastically. "The preacher says I should give until it hurts," said a miserly church member, "but for me, it hurts just to think about giving!" The Macedonian churches needed no prompting or reminding, as did the church at Corinth. They were more than willing to share in the collection. In fact, *they begged to be included!* (see v. 4). How many times have you heard Christians beg to take part in an offering?

Grace not only frees us from our sins, it also frees us from ourselves. The grace of God will open our heart *and our hand.* Our giving will not be the result of cold calculation, but of warm-hearted jubilation!

Applying God's Truth:

1. What are the most common excuses you hear people use for not giving more to their church?

2. In what ways do you think giving is related to God's grace in the life of the believer?

3. What three adjectives best describe your attitude toward giving?

Day 17

A "Poor" Example

Read 2 Corinthians 8:8–9

"You know the grace of our Lord Jesus Christ, that though he was rich, yet for your sakes he became poor, so that you through his poverty might become rich."

2 CORINTHIANS 8:9

In what ways was Jesus rich? Certainly He was rich in His person, for He is eternal God. He was rich in His possessions and in His position as King of kings and Lord of lords. He was rich in His power, for He can do anything. Yet, in spite of the fact that He had all these riches—and more—*He became poor.*

The tense of the verb indicates that it is His incarnation, His birth at Bethlehem, that is meant here. He united Himself to mankind and took upon Himself a human body. He left the throne to become a servant (see Phil. 2:7). He laid aside all His possessions so that He did not even have a place to lay His head (see Luke 9:58). His ultimate experience of poverty was when He was made to be sin for us on the cross (2 Cor. 5:21). Hell is eternal poverty, and on the cross Jesus Christ became the poorest of the poor.

Why did He do it? So that we might become rich! This suggests that we were poor before we met Jesus Christ, and we were—totally bankrupt. But now that we have trusted Him, we share in all of His riches! We are now the children of God, "heirs of God and co-heirs with Christ" (Rom. 8:17). Since this is true, *how can we refuse to give to others?* Jesus became poor to make us rich! Can we not follow His example (see 1 Peter 2:21)?

Applying God's Truth:

1. How could your becoming poorer (financially) help someone else become richer (spiritually)?

2. Why do you think Jesus chose to live a human life of poverty when He could just as easily have led a sinless but wealthy life?

3. In your opinion, how closely related are people's giving habits and their spiritual maturity?

Day 18

Heart Gifts

Read 2 Corinthians 8:10–24

*"Last year you were the first not only to give but also to have the
desire to do so. Now finish the work, so that your eager willingness
to do it may be matched by your completion of it."*

2 Corinthians 8:10–11

Grace giving must come from a willing heart; it cannot be coerced
or forced. During my years of ministry, I have endured many
offering appeals. I have listened to pathetic tales about unbelievable
needs. I have forced myself to laugh at old jokes that were supposed
to make it easier for me to part with my money. I have been scolded,
shamed, and almost threatened, and I must confess that none of these
approaches has ever stirred me to give more than I planned to give.
In fact, more than once I gave less because I was so disgusted with the
worldly approach. (However, I have never gotten like Mark Twain,
who said that he was so sickened by the long appeal that he not only
did not give what he planned to give but he took a bill out of the
plate!)

We must be careful here not to confuse *willing* with *doing*,
because the two must go together. If the willing is sincere and in the
will of God, then there must be a "completion of it" (v. 11; Phil.
2:12–13). Paul did not say that *willing* was a substitute for *doing*,
because it is not. But if our giving is motivated by grace, we will give
more willingly, and not because we have been forced to give.

God sees the "heart gift" and not the "hand gift." If the heart
wants to give more, but is unable to do so, God sees it and records it

accordingly. But if the hand gives more than the heart wants to give, God records what is in the heart, no matter how big the offering in the hand may be.

Applying God's Truth:

1. What fund-raising techniques are most offensive to you? Which, if any, do you endorse?

2. Do you think pastors ought to spend much time discussing giving to the church? Why or why not?

3. Do you think giving is an ongoing priority for most people, or do they tend to give in spurts? Why?

Day 19

Prompting Without Pressuring

Read 2 Corinthians 9:1–5

"I thought it necessary to urge the brothers to visit you in advance and finish the arrangements for the generous gift you had promised. Then it will be ready as a generous gift, not as one grudgingly given."

2 Corinthians 9:5

Apparently, Paul did not see anything wrong or unspiritual about asking people to promise to give. He did not tell them how much they had to promise, but he did expect them to keep their promise. Notice the words that Paul used as he wrote about the collection. It was a "service to the saints" (v. 1) and "a generous gift" (v. 5). Was Paul perhaps hinting that the Corinthians should give more than they had planned?

However, Paul was careful not to put on any pressure. He wanted their gift to be "a generous gift, not as one grudgingly given." High-pressure offering appeals do not belong to grace giving.

Our greatest encouragement for giving is that it pleases the Lord, but there is nothing wrong with practicing the kind of giving that provokes others to give. This does not mean that we should advertise what we do as individuals, because that kind of practice would violate one of the basic principles of giving: Give secretly to the Lord (see Matt. 6:1–4). However, Paul was writing to *churches,* and it is not wrong for congregations to announce what they have given collectively. If our motive is to boast, then we are not practicing grace giving. But if our desire is to provoke others to share, then God's grace can work through us to help others.

Applying God's Truth:

1. To what extent do you need to be prompted from time to time to give to your church?

2. If giving is to be done willingly, out of generosity, do you think it is improper to ask people to give? Why?

3. What are some ways to inspire people to give without having to ask them?

Day 20

Waiting for the Harvest

Read 2 Corinthians 9:6–15

> *"Remember this: Whoever sows sparingly will also reap sparingly,
> and whoever sows generously will also reap generously."*
>
> 2 CORINTHIANS 9:6

As we sow, we are enriched, and we enrich others (see v. 11). Farmers reap immediate physical benefits as they work in their fields, but they have to wait for the harvest. Christians who are motivated by grace reap the blessings of personal enrichment in their own life and character, and their enrichment benefits others. The final result is glory to God as others give thanks to Him. Paul was careful to point out that grace giving does not bring credit to us; it brings thanksgiving to God. We are but channels through whom God works to meet the needs of others.

God enriches us so that we may give even more bountifully (see vv. 8–11). One of the blessings of grace giving is the joy of giving more and more. Everything we have—not just our income—belongs to God, is given to God, and is used by God to accomplish His work. We are enriched in everything with Him and with others. As a pastor, I have watched young Christians lay hold of these principles of grace giving and start to grow. It has been a great joy to see them trust God as their giving is motivated by grace.

Grace giving means that we really believe that God is the great Giver, and we use our material and spiritual resources accordingly. We simply cannot outgive God!

Applying God's Truth:

1. Recall some personal examples that illustrate the sowing/reaping principle of 2 Corinthians 9:6.

2. When you give to the church, to what extent do you want to see definite (and perhaps immediate) results?

3. Do you think we see most of the "harvest" of our giving? Why or why not?

Day 21

Walls of Resistance

Read 2 Corinthians 10:1–6

> *"The weapons we fight with are not the weapons of the world.*
> *On the contrary, they have divine power to demolish strongholds.*
> *We ... take captive every thought to make it obedient to Christ."*

2 CORINTHIANS 10:4–5

There are walls of resistance in the minds of people, and these walls must be pulled down (see v. 4 KJV). What are these "mental walls"? Reasonings that are opposed to the truth of God's Word. Pride of intelligence that exalts itself. Paul was not attacking intelligence, but intellectualism, the high-minded attitude that makes people think they know more than they really do. Paul faced this "wisdom of men" when he founded the church (see 1 Cor. 1:18ff), and it surfaced again with the coming of the Judaizers.

Paul's attitude of humility was actually one of his strongest weapons, for pride plays right into the hands of Satan. The meek Son of God had far more power than Pilate (see John 19:11), and He proved it. To tear down the opposition, Paul used spiritual weapons—prayer, the Word of God, love, the power of the Spirit at work in his life. He did not depend on personality, human abilities, or even the authority he had as an apostle. However, he was ready to punish the offenders, if necessary, once the congregation had submitted to the Lord (see v. 6).

Many believers today do not realize that the church is involved in spiritual warfare, and those who do understand the seriousness of the Christian battle do not always know how to fight the battle. They try to use human methods to defeat demonic forces, and these methods are doomed to fail.

Applying God's Truth:

1. What are some of the "strongholds" that have positioned themselves in your life?

2. What are some spiritual "weapons" you may not be utilizing as well as you should? How can you use them more effectively?

3. What other "weapons" have you been using that simply haven't been getting the job done?

Day 22

Mature Authority

Read 2 Corinthians 10:7–11

"Even if I boast somewhat freely about the authority the Lord gave us for building you up rather than pulling you down, I will not be ashamed of it."

2 CORINTHIANS 10:8

In my many years of ministry, I have never ceased to be amazed at how some local churches treat their pastors. If a man shows love and true humility, they resist his leadership and break his heart. The next pastor may be a "dictator" who "runs the church"—and gets just what he wants. And the people love him and brag about him! Our Lord was treated the same way as the first pastor, so perhaps we should not be surprised.

The opponents in the church were accusing Paul of not being a true apostle; for, if he were a true apostle, he would show it by using his authority. On the other hand, if Paul had "thrown his weight around," they would have found fault with him for doing so. No matter what course Paul took, he was bound to be condemned. This is what happens when church members are not spiritually minded, but evaluate ministry from a worldly viewpoint.

How Christian leaders use authority is an evidence of their spiritual maturity and character. Immature leaders *swell* as they use their authority, but mature leaders *grow* in the use of authority, and others grow with them. Wise pastors, like wise parents, know when to wait in loving patience and when to act with determined power. It takes more power to wait than to strike. Mature pastors do not use authority to *demand* respect, but to *command* respect. Mature leaders suffer while they wait to act, while immature leaders act impetuously and make others suffer.

Applying God's Truth:

1. Do you think your pastor gets fair treatment from most congregation members? What problems, if any, do you detect?

2. How do you think pastors feel when they, like Paul, are forced to defend their ministries to insensitive accusers?

3. When you are in authority, do you tend to *command* respect or *demand* it?

Day 23

Test Time

Read 2 Corinthians 10:12–18

*"It is not the one who commends himself who is approved,
but the one whom the Lord commends."*

2 CORINTHIANS 10:18

How does God approve our work? By testing it. The Greek word translated "approved" in verse 18 means "approved by testing." There is a future testing at the Judgment Seat of Christ (see 1 Cor. 3:10ff), but there is also a present testing of the work that we do. God permits difficulties to come to local churches in order that their work might be tested and approved.

Over the years, I have seen ministries tested by financial losses, the invasion of false doctrine, the emergence of proud leaders who want to "run the church," and the challenge of change. Some of the churches have fallen apart and almost died because their work was not spiritual. Other ministries have grown because of their trials and have become purer and stronger, and, through it all, God was glorified.

Certainly our ministries must keep records and issue reports, but we must not fall into the "snare of statistics" and think that numbers are the only measurement of ministry. Each situation is unique, and no ministry can honestly be evaluated on the basis of some other ministry. The important thing is that we are where God wants us to be, doing what He wants us to do so that He might be glorified. Motive is as much a part of God's measurement of our work as is growth. If we are seeking to glorify and please God alone, and if we are not afraid of His evaluation of our hearts and lives, then we need not fear the estimates of people or their criticisms.

"Let him who boasts boast in the Lord" (2 Cor. 10:17).

Applying God's Truth:

1. What do you think of people who tend to commend themselves a lot? Why?

2. Do you think your church is ever in danger of falling into the "snare of statistics"? If so, in what ways?

3. What are some ways that God has recently "tested" *your* work? What were the results?

Day 24

Homeward Bound

Read 2 Corinthians 11:1–15

> *"I will keep on doing what I am doing in order to cut*
> *the ground from under those who want an opportunity*
> *to be considered equal with us in the things they boast about."*
>
> 2 Corinthians 11:12

Paul had not used any devious tricks to catch the believers by surprise, attack them, or rob them. Both in his preaching of the gospel and his handling of finances, he was open and honest. In my own travels, I have seen situations in local churches that have broken my heart. I have seen congregations show little or no appreciation to faithful pastors who were laboring sacrificially to see the churches grow. Some of these men were underpaid and overworked, yet the churches seemed to have no love for them. However, their successors were treated like kings!

I once heard Dr. W. A. Criswell tell about the faithful missionary couple who returned to the United States on the same ship that brought Teddy Roosevelt home from a safari in Africa. Many reporters and photographers were on the dock waiting to see Roosevelt and interview him and take pictures, but nobody was on hand to welcome home the veteran missionaries who had spent their lives serving Christ in Africa.

That evening, in their modest hotel room, the couple reviewed their arrival in New York City, and the husband was somewhat bitter.

"It isn't fair," he said to his wife. "Mr. Roosevelt comes home from a hunting trip, and the whole country is out to meet him. We get home after years of service, and nobody is there to greet us."

But his wife had the right answer: *"Honey, we aren't home yet."*

Applying God's Truth:

1. How do you feel when you hear others try to justify themselves by comparing themselves to other people when they have no genuine actions to back their claims? How do you think Paul felt?

2. Can you think of any current injustices in your own church where one person or group is being glorified when someone else is doing much more work?

3. In what ways are your own efforts being overlooked by others? How do you respond in such situations?

Day 25

Why Bother?

Read 2 Corinthians 11:16–33

"I have labored and toiled and have often gone without sleep;
I have known hunger and thirst and have often gone without food;
I have been cold and naked. Besides everything else, I face
daily the pressure of my concern for all the churches."

2 Corinthians 11:27–28

In my own limited itinerant ministry, I have had the convenience of automobiles and planes, and yet I must confess that travel wears me out. How much more difficult it was for Paul! No wonder he was filled with weariness and pain. He often had to go without food, drink, and sleep, and sometimes he lacked sufficient clothing to keep himself warm.

While any other traveler could have suffered these things, Paul endured them because of his love for Christ and the church. His greatest burden was not *around* him, but *within* him: "the care of all the churches" (v. 28 KJV). Why did he care so much? Because he identified with the believers (see v. 29). Whatever happened to his "children" (6:13) touched his own heart, and he could not abandon them.

Paul climaxed this narration of his sufferings by telling of his humiliating experience at Damascus, when he—the great apostle—was smuggled out of the city in a basket let over the wall! (see 11:32–33). Would any of the Judaizers ever tell a story like that about themselves? Of course not! Even when Paul did narrate his sufferings, he was careful that Christ was glorified, and not Paul. May we never take for granted the sacrifices that others have made so that we may enjoy the blessings of the gospel today.

Applying God's Truth:

1. What are some ways that you have suffered for the good of your church?

2. Think of all the people actively involved in your church. Can you think of anyone being overlooked who could use a note or word of encouragement?

3. If you and your fellow church members were willing to suffer a little more for the good of the church as a whole, what might be some of the results?

Day 26

A Secret and a Thorn

Read 2 Corinthians 12:1–6

"I know a man in Christ who fourteen years ago was caught up to the third heaven.... And I know that this man ... was caught up to paradise. He heard inexpressible things, things that man is not permitted to tell."

2 Corinthians 12:2–4

The interesting thing is that Paul kept quiet about this experience of heaven for fourteen years! During those years, he was buffeted by a "thorn in the flesh" (v. 7 KJV), and perhaps people wondered why he had such a burdensome affliction. The Judaizers *may* have adopted the views of Job's comforters and said, "This affliction is a punishment from God." (Actually, it was a *gift* from God.) Some of Paul's good friends may have tried to encourage him by saying, "Cheer up, Paul. One day you'll be in heaven!" Paul could have replied, "That's why I have this thorn—because I *went* to heaven!"

God honored Paul by granting him visions and revelations, and by taking him to heaven, but He honored him further by permitting him to hear "inexpressible things" while he was there. He overheard the divine secrets that are shared only in that holy place. These things could be spoken by God and by celestial beings, but they could not be spoken by humans.

Such an honor as this would have made most people very proud. Instead of keeping quiet for fourteen years, they would have immediately told the world and become famous. But Paul did not become proud. He simply told the truth—it was not empty boasting—and let the facts speak for themselves. His great concern was that nobody should rob God of the glory.

Applying God's Truth:

1. Has anything astonishing ever happened in your Christian life?

2. When you tell others of the things God has done for you, how do you ensure that God gets the glory for those things (rather than having others simply think that *you have* become a better person)?

3. How do you accept all the things God has done for you without becoming proud?

Day 27

Options for Suffering

Read 2 Corinthians 12:7–8

> *"To keep me from becoming conceited because of these surpassingly great revelations, there was given me a thorn in my flesh, a messenger of Satan, to torment me."*
>
> 2 CORINTHIANS 12:7

When God permits suffering to come into people's lives, there are several ways they can deal with it. Some people become bitter and blame God for robbing them of freedom and pleasure. Others just "give up" and fail to get any blessing out of the experience because they will not put any courage into it. Still others grit their teeth and put on a brave front, determined to "endure to the very end." While this is a courageous response, it usually drains them of the strength needed for daily living; and after a time, they may collapse.

Was Paul sinning when he prayed to be delivered from Satan's buffeting? I don't think so. It is certainly a normal thing for a Christian to ask God for deliverance from sickness and pain. God has not *obligated* Himself to heal every believer who prays, but He has encouraged us to bring our burdens and needs to Him. Paul did not know whether this "thorn in the flesh" was a temporary test from God or a permanent experience he would have to learn to live with.

There are those who would have us believe that an afflicted Christian is a disgrace to God. "If you are obeying the Lord and claiming all that you have in Christ," they say, "then you will never be sick." I have never found that teaching in the Bible. It is true that God promised the Jews special blessing and protection under the Old Covenant (see Deut. 7:12ff), but He never promised the New Testament believers freedom from sickness or suffering.

Applying God's Truth:

1. Do you have any type of ailment you consider a "thorn" from God?

2. Why do you think God sometimes allows His people to endure chronic physical suffering?

3. What guidelines do you use to determine when to be persistent in prayer and when to accept something as a "thorn"?

Day 28

Rising above Suffering

Read 2 Corinthians 12:9–21

> *"I will boast all the more gladly about my weaknesses, so that Christ's power may rest on me.... For when I am weak, then I am strong."*
>
> 2 CORINTHIANS 12:9–10

God does not give us His grace simply to help us "endure" our sufferings. God's grace should enable us to *rise above* our circumstances and feelings and cause our afflictions to work *for us* in accomplishing positive good. God wants to build our character so that we are more like our Savior.

What benefits did Paul receive because of his suffering? For one thing, he experienced the power of Christ in his life. God transformed Paul's weakness into strength. The word translated "rest" means "to spread a tent over." Paul saw his body as an "earthly tent" (5:1ff), but the glory of God had come into that tent and transformed it into a holy tabernacle.

Something else happened to Paul as a result of his suffering: He was able to glory in his infirmities. This does not mean that he preferred pain to health, but rather that he knew how to turn his infirmities into assets. What made the difference? The grace of God *and* the glory of God. Paul delighted in these trials and problems, not because he was psychologically unbalanced and enjoyed pain, but because he knew he was suffering for the sake of Jesus Christ (see v. 10). He was glorifying God by the way he accepted and handled the difficult experiences of life.

"It is a greater thing to pray for pain's conversion than its removal," wrote P. T. Forsyth, and this is true. Paul won the victory, not by substitution, but by transformation. He discovered the sufficiency of the grace of God (see v. 9).

Applying God's Truth:

1. What effect should God's grace have on the "thorns" in your life?

2. Paraphrase Paul's statement in verse 10 as if you were answering a friend's query: "How can weakness be a strength?"

3. How would your spiritual life be different if you focused more on "converting" pain than on having God completely remove it?

Day 29

Deceptive Strength

Read 2 Corinthians 13:1–10

"He is not weak in dealing with you, but is powerful among you. For to be sure, he was crucified in weakness, yet he lives by God's power."

2 Corinthians 13:3–4

L et Paul prove he is a true apostle!" said his opponents. Paul's reply was, "Like Jesus Christ, I am strong when it appears I am weak." On the cross, Jesus Christ manifested weakness; but the cross is still "the power of God" (1 Cor. 1:18). By the standards of the world, both Jesus and Paul were weak, but by the standards of the Lord, both were strong. It is a wise and mature worker who knows when to be "weak" and when to be "strong" in dealing with discipline problems in the local church.

A pastor friend of mine, now in heaven, had a quiet manner of delivery in the pulpit, and a similar approach in his personal ministry. After hearing him deliver a sermon, a visitor said, "I kept waiting for him to start preaching!" She was accustomed to hearing a loud preacher who generated more heat than light. But my friend built a strong church because he knew the true standards for ministry. He knew how to be "weak in Christ" and also how to be "strong."

How do we measure the ministry today? By powerful oratory or biblical content? By Christian character or what the press releases say? Too many times we Christians follow the world's standards when we evaluate ministries; instead, we need to pay attention to God's standards.

Applying God's Truth:

1. What are some ways that Jesus was strong when He appeared weak?

2. Do you think some of your own strengths are interpreted by others as weaknesses? If so, in what ways?

3. Would you say your personal ministry generates more "heat" or more "light"?

Day 30

Be (and Stay) Encouraged

Read 2 Corinthians 13:11–14

"Aim for perfection, listen to my appeal, be of one mind, live in peace.
And the God of love and peace will be with you."

2 CORINTHIANS 13:11

Our God is the "God of love and peace." Can the outside world tell that from the way we Christians live and conduct the business of the church? "Behold how they love one another!" was what the lost world said about the early church, but it has been a long time since the church has earned that kind of commendation.

Like Christians today, the Corinthian believers desperately needed the blessings of grace, love, and communion. Just as cultists do today, the Judaizers emphasized law instead of grace, exclusiveness instead of love, and independence rather than communion (fellowship). The competition in the Corinthian church, resulting in divisions, would have been eliminated if the people had only lived by God's grace and love.

The church is a miracle, and it can be sustained only by the miracle ministry of God. No amount of human skill, talents, or programs can make the church what it ought to be. Only God can do that. If each of us believers is depending on the grace of God, walking in the love of Christ, and participating in the fellowship of the Spirit, not walking in the flesh, then we will be a part of the answer and not a part of the problem. We will be *living* this benediction—and *being* a benediction to others! Ask God to make you that kind of Christian.

Be encouraged and then encourage others.

Applying God's Truth:

1. If a stranger monitored your words and actions for a week, do you think that person would think you serve "a God of love and peace"?

2. What things do you do to try to build unity with other believers?

3. What three things could someone do for you (or say to you) that would encourage you most?

Maturity

Thirty Daily Readings from the Book of James

There is a vast difference between age and maturity. Not everybody who grows old grows up.

Age is a quantity of time; maturity is a quality of experience. Age happens automatically: Those who have the most birthdays live the longest. But maturity isn't automatic; people have to work at it.

Mature people have more life and enjoy more of life, especially the Christian life. God didn't save us from our sins in order to keep us infants in His family. He saved us so we would grow up and become more like Jesus Christ. Only then can we glorify Him and serve others. It is a tough world we live in, and we can't make it through successfully without maturity.

Mature Christians aren't *learners*, always depending on somebody else to bail them out and carry them through. Instead, they are *leaders* who trust Christ to give them the encouragement and empowerment they need for the demands of life. Through Jesus Christ, they can face life courageously and make it work *for* them, not *against* them.

For mature Christians, life is not a playground in which babies fight over toys; it is a battleground where great moral issues must be defended. God can't send babies into battle. That's why He is challenging you and me to be mature, to develop the kind of Christian character that can stand the test.

The epistle of James is about maturity, Christian maturity. It describes the characteristics of mature Christians and explains how they got that way. James also explains the important role that trials play in a maturing life, and he shows us how to keep our life in balance. (Infants are prone to stumble.) He even devotes an entire chapter to the question, "Why can't people get along with each other?"

Each of us is either a part of the problem or a part of the answer. Mature Christians—and that includes *you*—are part of the answer.

Day 1

Meet the Author

Read James 1:1

> *"James, a servant of God and of the Lord Jesus Christ,*
> *To the twelve tribes scattered among the nations: Greetings."*
>
> JAMES 1:1

James, the brother of our Lord, seems to be the most likely candidate for author of this letter. (By "brother," of course, I mean half brother; Joseph was not our Lord's father since Jesus was conceived by the Holy Spirit of God.)

James and the other brothers did not believe in Jesus during His earthly ministry (see John 7:1–5 and Mark 3:31–35). Yet we find our Lord's brethren in the upper room praying with the disciples (see Acts 1:14). What effected the change from unbelief to faith? First Corinthians 15:7 indicates that Jesus appeared to James after His resurrection! This appearance convinced James that Jesus truly was the Savior, and he, in turn, shared this knowledge about Jesus with the other brothers.

James became the leader of the church in Jerusalem. Paul called him a pillar (see Gal. 2:9). It was James who moderated the church conference described in Acts 15. He must have been a deeply spiritual man to gain the leadership of the Jerusalem church in such a short time. His stature is seen in Acts 15, where he was able to permit all the factions to express themselves and then bring peace by drawing a conclusion based on the Word of God.

Applying God's Truth:

1. Have you ever been amazed at the accomplishments of a family member or close friend? How do you think James felt to discover that his brother was actually the Savior of the world?

2. An encounter with the resurrected Jesus turned James's life around. In what ways has your life changed due to your discoveries about who Jesus really is?

3. What are some of your goals as you read through these devotions from the book of James?

Day 2

Great Expectations

Read James 1:2

"Consider it pure joy, my brothers, whenever you face trials of many kinds."

JAMES 1:2

Outlook determines outcome, and attitude determines action. God tells us to expect trials. Believers who expect the Christian life to be easy are in for a shock. Because we are God's *scattered* people (see v. 1) and not His *sheltered* people, we must experience trials. We cannot always expect everything to go our way. Some trials come simply because we are human—sickness, accidents, disappointments, even seeming tragedies. Other trials come because we are Christians. Satan fights us, the world opposes us, and this conflict makes for a life of battle.

My wife and I once visited a world-famous weaver and watched his men and women work on the looms. I noticed that the undersides of the rugs were not very beautiful: The patterns were obscure, and the loose ends of the yarn dangled. "Don't judge the worker or the work by looking at the wrong side," our guide told us. In the same way, we are looking at the wrong side of life; only the Lord sees the finished pattern. Let's not judge Him or His work from what we see today. His work is not finished yet!

Applying God's Truth:

1. What are some of the more severe trials you are facing right now?

2. How many of your trials can you honestly say you are facing with "pure joy"? How can you glean more joy out of your less-than-desirable circumstances?

3. Do you tend to think God is uncaring or unfair when you have to experience unpleasant or undesired circumstances? Why?

Day 3

On Trial

Read James 1:3

> *"You know that the testing of your faith develops perseverance."*
> JAMES 1:3

The only way the Lord can develop patience and character in our lives is through trials. Endurance cannot be attained by reading a book, listening to a sermon, or even praying a prayer. We must go through the difficulties of life, trust God, and obey Him. The result will be patience and character. Knowing this truth, we can face trials joyfully. We know that the end result will bring glory to God.

This fact explains why studying the Bible helps us grow in patience (see Rom. 15:4). As we read about Abraham, Joseph, Moses, David, and even our Lord, we realize that God has a purpose in trials. God fulfills His purposes as we trust Him. There is no substitute for an understanding mind. Satan can defeat ignorant believers, but he cannot overcome Christians who know the Bible and understand the purposes of God.

Applying God's Truth:

1. How do athletes develop perseverance on a physical level? How do we Christians develop *spiritual* perseverance?

2. What Bible character do you think best demonstrates perseverance? Why? What can you learn from that person?

3. Rather than complain the next time your faith is tested, what are some other options you could try instead?

Day 4

A Common Problem

Read James 1:4

> *"Perseverance must finish its work so that you may be mature and complete, not lacking anything."*
>
> JAMES 1:4

As we read the epistle of James, we discover that the Jewish Christians were having some problems in their personal lives and in their church fellowship. For one thing, they were going through some difficult tests. They were also facing temptations to sin. Some of the believers were catering to the rich, while others were being robbed by the rich. Church members were competing for offices in the church, particularly teaching offices.

One of the major problems in the church was a failure on the part of many to live what they professed to believe. Furthermore, the tongue was a serious problem, even to the point of creating wars and divisions in the assembly. Worldliness was another problem. Some of the members were disobeying God's Word and were sick physically because of it, and some were straying away from the Lord and the church.

But James was not discussing an array of miscellaneous problems. All of these problems had a common cause: *spiritual immaturity.* These Christians simply were not growing up. This gives us a hint as to the basic theme of this letter: *the marks of maturity in the Christian life.*

Applying God's Truth:

1. On a scale of 1 (least) to 10 (most), what would you say is your current level of spiritual maturity? Why?

2. Think back to your life one year ago. How have you matured spiritually since that time?

3. What is the significance of perseverance in the development of spiritual maturity?

Day 5

Wisdom in Action

Read James 1:5–11

> *"If any of you lacks wisdom, he should ask God, who gives generously to all without finding fault, and it will be given to him."*
>
> JAMES 1:5

Wisdom is the right use of knowledge. All of us know people who are educated fools: They have brilliant academic records, but they cannot make the simplest decisions in life. I once met a gifted professor on a seminary campus, and he was wearing two hats!

Why do we need wisdom when we are going through trials? Why not ask for strength, or grace, or even deliverance? For this reason: *We need wisdom so we will not waste the opportunities God is giving us to mature.* Wisdom helps us understand how to use these circumstances for our good and God's glory.

An associate of mine, a gifted secretary, was going through great trials. She had had a stroke, her husband had gone blind, and then he had to be taken to the hospital where (we were sure) he would die. I saw her in church one Sunday and assured her that I was praying for her.

"What are you asking God to do?" she asked, and her question startled me.

"I'm asking God to help you and strengthen you," I replied.

"I appreciate that," she said, "but pray about one more thing. Pray that I'll have the wisdom not to waste all of this!"

She knew the meaning of James 1:5.

Applying God's Truth:

1. How would you define "wisdom" from a biblical perspective to a friend who might ask?

2. What are some problems you are facing today for which you need to request God's wisdom?

3. Since God "gives [wisdom] generously to all without finding fault," why do you think so many Christians are confused as to His will for their lives?

Day 6

Beware the Hook

Read James 1:12–15

"When tempted, no one should say, 'God is tempting me.' For God cannot be tempted by evil, nor does he tempt anyone; but each one is tempted when, by his own evil desire, he is dragged away and enticed."

JAMES 1:13–14

No temptation appears as temptation; it always seems more alluring than it really is. James used two illustrations from the world of outdoor sports to prove his point. In the original Greek, "dragged away" carries with it the idea of the baiting of a trap, and "enticed" suggests the baiting of a hook. The hunter and the fisher have to use bait to attract and catch their prey. No animal is deliberately going to step into a trap, and no fish will knowingly bite at a naked hook. The idea is *to hide* the trap and the hook.

Temptation always carries with it some bait that appeals to our natural desires. The bait not only attracts us, it also hides the fact that yielding to the desire will eventually bring us sorrow and punishment. It is the bait that is the exciting thing.

When Jesus was tempted by the Devil in Luke 4:1–13, He dealt with the temptation on the basis of the Word of God. Three times He said, "It is written," or "It says" (vv. 4, 8, 12). From the human point of view, turning stones into bread to satisfy hunger is a sensible thing to do, as Jesus was tempted to do in verse 3, but not from God's point of view. When we know the Bible, we can detect the bait and deal with it decisively. This is what it means to walk by faith and not by sight (see 2 Cor. 5:7 KJV).

Applying God's Truth:

1. Are there certain areas in which you seem more prone to temptation than other areas? What are they, and how do you try to deal with recurring temptations in those particularly vulnerable areas?

2. How would you differentiate between the fact that God allows tests of our faith (see 1:3), yet never tempts us (see 1:13)?

3. If someone wanted to tempt you to do wrong, what "bait" would that person use? Whenever you see that "bait," have you trained yourself to look for the "hook" as well?

Day 7

Bright Forecast

Read James 1:16–18

"Every good and perfect gift is from above, coming down from the Father
of the heavenly lights, who does not change like shifting shadows."

JAMES 1:17

There are no shadows with the Father of lights. It is impossible for God to change. He cannot change for the worse because He is holy; He cannot change for the better because He is perfect. The light of the sun varies as the earth changes, but the sun itself is still shining. If shadows come between the Father and us, He did not cause them. He is the unchanging God. This means that we should never question His love or doubt His goodness when difficulties come or temptations appear.

The first barrier against temptation is a negative one: the judgment of God. The second barrier is positive: the goodness of God. A fear of God is a healthy attitude, but the love of God must balance it. We can obey Him because He may chasten us; or we can obey Him because He has already been so generous to us, and because we love Him for it.

The next time you are tempted, meditate on the goodness of God in your life. If you think you need something, wait for the Lord to provide it. Never toy with the Devil's bait. One reason God allows us to be tempted is to teach us patience. David was tempted twice to kill King Saul and hasten his own coronation (see 1 Sam. chaps. 24 and 26), but he resisted the temptation and waited for God's time.

Applying God's Truth:

1. Do you ever wish God would give you something *better* than what you have received from Him? If so, what do you think James would say about such thinking?

2. What are some things that occasionally get between you and God and tend to form "shadows"?

3. Are you completely, totally convinced of the absolute goodness of God? If not, what can you do to get a clearer perspective of His goodness?

Day 8

Two to One

Read James 1:19–20

"Everyone should be quick to listen, slow to speak and slow to become angry,
for man's anger does not bring about the righteous life that God desires"
JAMES 1:19–20

We have two ears and one mouth, which ought to remind us to listen more than we speak. Too many times we argue with God's Word, if not audibly, at least in our hearts and minds.

We should not get angry with God or His Word. "A patient man has great understanding, but a quick-tempered man displays folly" (Prov. 14:29). Many church fights are the result of short tempers and hasty words. There is a godly anger against sin, and if we love the Lord, we must hate sin. But our anger does not produce God's righteousness. In fact, anger is just the opposite of the patience God wants to produce in our lives as we mature in Christ.

I once saw a poster that read, "Temper is such a valuable thing, it is a shame to lose it!" It is temper that helps to give steel its strength. If we cannot get angry at sin, we will not have much strength to fight it. James warns us against getting angry with God's Word because His Word reveals our sins to us. Like the man who broke the mirror because he disliked the image in it, we rebel against God's Word because it tells the truth about us and our sinfulness.

Applying God's Truth:

1. When was the last time you became really angry? Do you think the situation would have been different if you had been quicker to listen and slower to speak?

2. In what ways do people tend to get angry with others in an attempt to "bring about the righteous life that God desires"?

3. If anger is not a good solution to such situations, what are some better ones?

Day 9

Crop Failure?

Read James 1:21

> *"Get rid of all moral filth and the evil that is so prevalent and humbly accept the word planted in you, which can save you."*
>
> JAMES 1:21

James sees the human heart as a garden; if left to itself, the soil will produce only weeds. He urges us to "pull out the weeds" and prepare the soil for the "implanted Word of God." He gives the picture of a garden overgrown with weeds that cannot be controlled. It is foolish to try to receive God's Word into an unprepared heart.

How do we prepare the soil of our hearts for God's Word? First, by confessing our sins and asking the Father to forgive us. Then, by meditating on God's love and grace and asking Him to "plow up" any hardness in our hearts. Finally, we must have an attitude of meekness. When we receive the Word with humility, we accept it, do not argue with it, and honor it as the Word of God. We do not try to twist it to conform it to our thinking.

If we do not receive the implanted Word, then we are deceiving ourselves. If we like to argue various "points of view," we may be only fooling ourselves. We may think that our "discussions" are promoting spiritual growth, when in reality they may only be cultivating the weeds.

Applying God's Truth:

1. What are some of the "weeds" you have eliminated from your life since becoming a Christian? Do they tend to grow back, or have you pulled them up by the roots?

2. What are some other weeds you are still having to deal with?

3. In preparing your heart to receive God's Word, what do you find most difficult to do?

Day 10

Through the Looking Glass

Read James 1:23–27

> *"Anyone who listens to the word but does not do what it says is like a man who looks at his face in a mirror and, after looking at himself, goes away and immediately forgets what he looks like."*

JAMES 1:23–24

The main purpose for owning a mirror is to be able to see ourselves and make ourselves look as clean and neat as possible. As we look into the mirror of God's Word, we see ourselves as we really are. James mentions several mistakes that we make as we look into God's mirror.

First, *we merely glance at ourselves*. We do not carefully study ourselves as we read the Word. Many times we believers read a chapter of the Bible each day, but it is only a religious exercise, and we fail to profit from it personally. Our conscience would bother us if we did not have our daily Bible reading, when actually our conscience should bother us because *we read the Word carelessly*.

The second mistake is that *we forget what we see*. If we were looking deeply enough into our hearts, what we would see would be unforgettable.

Mistake number three is: *We fail to obey what the Word tells us to do*. We think that hearing is the same as doing, and it is not. We Christians enjoy substituting reading for doing, or even talking for doing.

If we are to use God's mirror profitably, then we must gaze into it carefully and with serious intent. No quick glances will do. We must examine our own hearts and lives in the light of God's Word. This requires time, attention, and sincere devotion. Five minutes with God each day will never constitute a deep spiritual examination.

Applying God's Truth:

1. How do you think your life would be different if mirrors had never been invented?

2. In your own experience, which of the three mistakes do you tend to make most frequently?

3. How can you restructure your devotional times in order to look more intently into the mirror of God's Word?

Day 11

Outer Appearances

Read James 2:1–4

*"My brothers, as believers in our glorious
Lord Jesus Christ, don't show favoritism."*

JAMES 2:1

The religious experts in Christ's day judged Him by their human standards, and they rejected Him. He came from the wrong city, Nazareth of Galilee. He was not a graduate of their accepted schools. He did not have the official approval of the people in power. He had no wealth. His followers were a nondescript mob and included publicans and sinners. *Yet he was the very glory of God.*

Sad to say, we often make the same mistakes. When visitors come into our churches, we tend to judge them on what we see outwardly rather than what they are inwardly. Dress, color of skin, fashion, and other superficial things carry more weight than the fruit of the Spirit that may be manifest in their lives. We cater to the rich because we hope to get something out of them, and we avoid the poor because they embarrass us. Jesus did not engage in such discrimination, and He cannot approve of it.

How do we practice the deity of Christ in our human relationships? It is really quite simple: by *looking at everyone through the eyes of Christ.* If visitors are Christians, we can accept them because Christ lives in them. If they are not Christians, we can receive them because Christ died for them. It is Christ who is the link between us and others, and He is a link of love. The basis for relationship with others is the person and work of Jesus Christ. Any other basis is not going to work.

Applying God's Truth:

1. Have you ever been a victim of discrimination? In what ways? Have you ever experienced *spiritual* discrimination?

2. Can you think of ways your church may tend to show favoritism to certain individuals or groups? Is there anything you can do about it?

3. Try this experiment: Attempt to see the next three people you come into contact with as you think Jesus would see those people. Make a mental note of any new observations you discover.

Day 12

Law and Love

Read James 2:5–9

> *"If you really keep the royal law found in Scripture, 'Love your neighbor as yourself,' you are doing right. But if you show favoritism, you sin and are convicted by the law as lawbreakers."*
>
> JAMES 2:8–9

Showing respect of persons can lead us into disobeying all of God's law. Take any one of the Ten Commandments, and we will find ways of breaking it if we respect other people's social or financial status. Respect of persons could make us lie, for example. It could lead to idolatry (getting money out of the rich), or even mistreatment of our parents. Once we start acting on the basis of respecting persons and rejecting God's Word, we are heading for trouble. And we need not break *all* of God's law to be guilty (see v. 10). There is only one Lawgiver, and all of His laws are from His mind and heart. If we disobey one law, we are capable of disobeying all of them; and by rebelling, we have already done so.

Christian love does not mean that we must *like* other people and agree with them on everything. We may not like their vocabulary or their habits, and we may not want them as intimate friends. *Christian love means treating others the way God has treated us.* It is an act of the will, not an emotion that we try to manufacture. The motive is to glorify God. The means is the power of the Holy Spirit within us. As we act in love toward others, we may find ourselves drawn more and more to them, and we may see in them (through Christ) qualities that before were hidden to us.

Applying God's Truth:

1. What are some excuses you have heard people give to justify disobedience to God's clear commands?

2. Can you identify any ways in which your own "respect of persons" somehow interferes with your spiritual commitment?

3. Do you think it is possible to love people you don't particularly like? Explain.

Day 13

License and Liberty

Read James 2:10–13

> *"Speak and act as those who are going to be judged by the law that gives freedom, because judgment without mercy will be shown to anyone who has not been merciful. Mercy triumphs over judgment!"*

JAMES 2:12–13

Liberty does not mean license. License (doing whatever we want to do) is the worst kind of bondage. Liberty means the freedom to be all that we can be in Jesus Christ. License is confinement; liberty is fulfillment.

The Word is called "the law that gives freedom" because God sees our hearts and knows what we would do if we were free to do so. If we obey God only because of His rules, we are not really maturing as Christians. What would we do if there were no rules? God's Word can change our hearts and give us the desire to do God's will, so that we obey from inward compulsion and not outward constraint.

There is one obvious message to this section: Our beliefs should control our behavior. If we really believe that Jesus is the Son of God, and that God is gracious, His Word is true, and one day He will judge us, then our conduct will reveal our convictions. Before we attack those who do not have orthodox doctrine, we must be sure that we practice the doctrines we defend. Jonah had wonderful theology, but he hated people and was angry with God (see Jonah 4).

One of the tests of the reality of our faith is how we treat other people. Can we pass the test?

Applying God's Truth:

1. In what ways does mercy triumph over judgment?

2. What are some ways that you exercise your Christian liberty? Do you ever catch yourself trying to use a spiritual "license" to do something you shouldn't?

3. If a stranger observed your behavior for a week, do you think that person could accurately determine your beliefs? Explain.

Day 14

Dead Faith

Read James 2:14–19

> *"What good is it, my brothers, if a man claims to have faith*
> *but has no deeds? Can such faith save him?"*
>
> JAMES 2:14

People with dead faith substitute words for deeds. They know the correct vocabulary for prayer and testimony, and can even quote the right verses from the Bible, but their walk does not measure up to their talk. They think that their words are as good as works, and they are wrong.

James gives a simple illustration in verses 15–16. A poor believer comes into a fellowship without proper clothing and in need of food. The person with dead faith notices the visitor and sees his needs but does nothing to meet the needs. All he does is say a few pious words! "Go, I wish you well; keep warm and well fed" (v. 16). But the visitor goes away just as hungry and naked as when he came in.

As believers, we have an obligation to help meet the needs of people, no matter who they may be. "As we have opportunity, let us do good to all people, especially to those who belong to the family of believers" (Gal. 6:10). Jesus has said, "I tell you the truth, whatever you did for one of the least of these brothers of mine, you did for me" (Matt. 25:40). To help a person in need is an expression of love, and faith works by love (see Gal. 5:6 KJV).

Applying God's Truth:

1. When was the last time you needed action from a person and received only words instead? How did you feel?

2. Do you think James is discounting the importance of faith by emphasizing actions so much? Why or why not?

3. Can you think of a time recently when *you* might have acted to help someone, yet settled for some kind of verbal affirmation instead? How can you prevent this incident from becoming a habit?

Day 15

Dynamic Faith

Read James 2:20–26

"As the body without the spirit is dead, so faith without deeds is dead."
James 2:26

Faith is only as good as its object. Primitive tribal people may have bowed before idols of stone and trusted them for help, but they received no such help. No matter how much faith such people may have generated, if it was not directed at the right object, it accomplished nothing. "I believe" may be the testimony of many sincere people today, but the big question is, "In whom do they believe? What do they believe?" People are not saved by *faith in faith;* they are saved by faith in Christ as revealed in God's Word.

Dynamic faith is based on God's Word, and true saving faith involves the whole person. The mind understands the truth, the heart desires the truth, and the will acts upon the truth. The men and women of faith named in Hebrews 11 were people of action: God spoke, and they obeyed. Again, faith is not believing in spite of *evidence;* faith is obeying in spite of *consequence.*

True saving faith *leads to action.* Dynamic faith is not intellectual contemplation or emotional consternation; it leads to obedience on the part of the will. And this obedience is not an isolated event; it continues throughout the whole life. It leads to works.

Applying God's Truth:

1. List several things or people that you have faith in, and then rate them from "most reliable" to "least reliable."

2. Think of a time recently when you had the faith to "obey in spite of consequence." What happened as a result?

3. Do you think most people are capable of increasing their actions for God without increasing their faith? What do you think would be likely to happen as a result of trying to act without true, dynamic faith?

Day 16

It Only Takes a Spark

Read James 3:1–6

*"The tongue also is a fire, a word of evil among the parts
of the body. It corrupts the whole person, sets the whole course
of his life on fire, and is itself set on fire by hell."*

JAMES 3:6

I was visiting the used bookstores along Charing Cross Road in London, and I remarked to a clerk that there were not as many stores as I expected. "There's a reason for that," he replied. "One night during World War II, the incendiary bombs hit, and the fires destroyed at least a million books!"

On another occasion, a friend was taking my wife and me on a tour of the beautiful forests in California, and we came to an ugly section that was burned out. Not only was the face of nature scarred, but millions of dollars of valuable timber had been wiped out. "Somebody's lit cigarette," my friend commented as we drove past the blackened earth.

A fire can begin with just a small spark, but it can grow to destroy a city. A fire reportedly started in the O'Leary barn in Chicago at 8:30 p.m., October 8, 1871; and because that fire spread, more than 100,000 people were left homeless, 17,500 buildings were destroyed, and 300 people died. It cost the city more than $400,000,000.

Our words can start fires. In some churches, there are members or officers who cannot control their tongues, and the result is destruction. Let them move out of town or be replaced in office, and a beautiful spirit of harmony and love often takes over.

Applying God's Truth:

1. In what ways have you experienced the destructive "fire" of someone else's harsh or insensitive words?

2. When was the last time you started a "four-alarm" verbal fire of your own? What was the issue that started it, and what were the results?

3. Since the tongue is a fire, what qualities do you need to have at your disposal as "spiritual fire extinguishers"?

Day 17

Tongue Taming

Read James 3:7–8

"No man can tame the tongue. It is a restless evil, full of deadly poison."
JAMES 3:8

Not only is the tongue like a fire, it is also like a dangerous animal. It is restless and cannot be ruled, and it seeks its prey and then pounces and kills. My wife and I once drove through a safari park, admiring the animals as they moved about in their natural habitat. But there were warning signs posted all over the park: DO NOT LEAVE YOUR CAR! DO NOT OPEN YOUR WINDOWS! Those "peaceful" animals were capable of doing great damage, and even killing.

Some animals are poisonous, and some tongues spread poison. The deceptive thing about poison is that it works secretly and slowly, and then it kills. How many times has some malicious person injected a bit of poison into the conversation, hoping it would spread and finally get to the person the talebearer wanted to hurt? As a pastor, I have seen poisonous tongues do great damage to individuals, families, classes, and entire churches. Would you turn hungry lions or angry snakes loose in your Sunday morning service? Of course not! But unruly tongues accomplish the same results.

James reminds us that animals can be tamed; and, for that matter, fire can be tamed. When we tame an animal, we get a worker instead of a destroyer. When we control fire, we generate power. The tongue cannot be tamed by man, but it can be tamed by God.

Applying God's Truth:

1. Based on your words during the past week, to what kind of animal(s) could you accurately compare your tongue?

2. Why is controlling our words particularly important in the context of church services?

3. In what ways do you think God "tames the tongue"? Do you think He can do so without our cooperation?

Day 18

Mixed Messages

Read James 3:9–12

*"Out of the same mouth come praise and cursing.
My brothers, this should not be."*

JAMES 3:10

If you and I are going to have tongues that delight, then we must meet with the Lord each day and learn from Him. We must get our "spiritual roots" deep into His Word. We must pray and meditate and permit the Holy Spirit to fill our hearts with God's love and truth.

But James issued a warning: A spring cannot give forth two kinds of water, and a tree cannot bear two different kinds of fruit (see vv. 11–12). We expect the spring to flow with fresh water at all times, and we expect the fig tree to bear figs and the olive tree to bear olives. Nature reproduces after its own kind.

If the tongue is inconsistent, there is something radically wrong with the heart. I heard about a professing Christian who got angry on the job and let loose with some oaths. Embarrassed, he turned to his partner and said, "I don't know why I said that. It really isn't in me." His partner wisely replied, "It had to be in you, or it couldn't have come out of you."

The tongue that praises the Father, and then turns around and curses men made in God's likeness (see v. 9), is in desperate need of spiritual medicine! How easy it is to sing the hymns during the worship service, then after the service, get into the family car and argue and fight all the way home! "My brothers, this should not be."

Applying God's Truth:

1. Can you think of any believers whose "inconsistent" tongues significantly damage their personal ministry?

2. Think of your comments to others so far today. What percentage of them were "fresh water"? What percentage were "salt water" (or bitter)?

3. Can you think of any recent comment you made about someone for which you need to go back to the person and apologize or otherwise make restitution?

Day 19

Knowledge versus Wisdom

Read James 3:13–17

"The wisdom that comes from heaven is first of all pure; then peace-loving, considerate, submissive, full of mercy and good fruit, impartial and sincere."

<small>JAMES 3:17</small>

Certainly, there is a great deal of knowledge in this world, and we all benefit from it; but there is not much wisdom. Man unlocks the secrets of the universe, but he does not know what to do with them. Almost everything he discovers or devises turns against him. More than a century ago, Henry David Thoreau warned that man had "improved means to unimproved ends."

Whenever I ride a bus or elevated train in the city, I often think of the man in Boston who was entertaining a famous Chinese scholar. He met his Oriental friend at the train station and rushed him to the subway. As they hurried through the subway station, the host panted to his guest, "If we run and catch this next train, we will save three minutes!" To which the patient Chinese philosopher replied, "And what significant thing shall we do with the three minutes we are saving?"

Man's wisdom is foolishness to God (see 1 Cor. 1:20), and God's wisdom is foolishness to man (see 2:14). Man's wisdom comes from reason, while God's wisdom comes from revelation. Man's worldly wisdom will come to nothing (see 1:19), while God's wisdom will endure forever.

Applying God's Truth:

1. What is some "wisdom of the world" you have heard or read lately that conflicts with God's wisdom?

2. What do you think are the primary sources of worldly wisdom?

3. On a scale of 1 (least) to 10 (most), rate your levels of wisdom according to each of the following standards: purity, peace-producing, consideration of others, submission, mercy, impartiality, and sincerity.

Day 20

Sowing and Reaping

Read James 3:18

"Peacemakers who sow in peace raise a harvest of righteousness."
JAMES 3:18

The Christian life is a life of sowing and reaping. For that matter, *every* life is a life of sowing and reaping, and we reap just what we sow (see Gal. 6:7–8). If we obey God's wisdom, we sow righteousness, not sin; and peace, not war. The life we live enables the Lord to bring righteousness and peace into the lives of others.

What we are is what we live, and what we live is what we sow. What we sow determines what we reap. If we live in God's wisdom, we sow righteousness and peace, and we reap God's blessing. If we live in worldly wisdom, we sow sin and war, and we reap "disorder and every evil practice" (James 3:16).

It is a serious thing to be a troublemaker in God's family. One of the sins that God hates is that of sowing "dissension among brothers" (see Prov. 6:16–19). Lot followed the world's wisdom and brought trouble to the camp of Abraham, but Abraham followed God's wisdom and brought peace. Abraham's decision, in the wisdom of God, led to blessings for his own household and ultimately for the whole world (see Gen. 13).

"Blessed is the man who finds wisdom, the man who gains understanding" (Prov. 3:13).

Applying God's Truth:

1. In what ways have you attempted to "sow in peace" lately?

2. What do you think is the connection between sowing *in peace* and harvesting *righteousness?*

3. Who is the best peacemaker you know? What can you learn from that person to become a better peacemaker yourself?

Day 21

At War with Ourselves

Read James 4:1–6

> *"You do not have, because you do not ask God. When you ask,
> you do not receive, because you ask with wrong motives,
> that you may spend what you get on your pleasures."*
>
> JAMES 4:2–3

The war in the heart is helping to cause the wars in the church! (See v. 1.)

The essence of sin is selfishness. Selfish desires are dangerous things. They lead to *wrong actions,* and they even lead to *wrong praying.* When our praying is wrong, our whole Christian life is wrong. It has well been said that the purpose of prayer is not to get our will done in heaven, but to get God's will done on earth.

Sometimes we use prayer as a cloak to hide our true desires. "But I prayed about it!" can be one of the biggest excuses we can use. Instead of seeking God's will, we tell God what He is supposed to do; and we get angry with Him if He does not obey. This anger at God eventually spills over, and we get angry with God's people. More than one church split has been caused by saints who take out their frustrations with God on the members of the church. Many a church or family problem would be solved if people would only look into their own hearts and see the battle raging there.

Applying God's Truth:

1. Can you recall a time when selfish desires led to wrong actions? What did you learn from the experience?

2. Can you think of any times when you may have prayed with improper motives? What led you to eventually discover your selfish motives?

3. What are some things you don't have that you need to ask God for? How can you keep your motives pure as you ask God to provide for your needs?

Day 22

Closing the Distance

Read James 4:7–12

> *"Submit yourselves ... to God. Resist the devil, and he will flee from you. Come near to God and he will come near to you."*
>
> JAMES 4:7-8

D r. A. W. Tozer has a profound essay in one of his books entitled, "Nearness Is Likeness." The more we are like God, the nearer we are to God. I may be sitting in my living room with my Siamese cat on my lap, and my wife may be twenty feet away in the kitchen; yet I am nearer to my wife than to the cat because the cat is unlike me. We have very little in common.

God graciously draws near to us when we deal with the sin in our lives that keeps Him at a distance. He will not share us with anyone else; He must have complete control. If we are double-minded (see v. 8), we can never be close to God.

It is possible to submit outwardly and yet not be humbled inwardly. God hates the sin of pride; if we are proud He will chasten us until we are humbled. We have a tendency to treat sin too lightly, even to laugh about it. But sin is serious, and one mark of true humility is facing the seriousness of sin and dealing with our disobedience.

Sometimes we hear a believer pray, "O Lord, humble me!" That is a dangerous thing to pray. Far better that we humble ourselves before God, confess our sins, weep over them, and turn from them (see vv. 9–10).

Applying God's Truth:

1. What are some ways that you try to "come near to God"? Which ones seem to work best for you?

2. How difficult do you find it to "resist the devil"? What methods do you use?

3. Do you try hard to humble yourself and get as close to God as possible, or do you feel safer or more comfortable when God seems to be at a distance?

Day 23

Countdown

Read James 4:13–14

"You do not even know what will happen tomorrow. What is your life? You are a mist that appears for a little while and then vanishes."

JAMES 4:14

We count our *years* at each birthday, but God tells us to number our *days* (see Ps. 90:12). After all, we live a day at a time, and those days rush by quickly the older we grow.

Since life is so brief, we cannot afford merely to "spend our lives"; and we certainly do not want to "waste our lives." We must invest our lives in those things that are eternal.

God reveals His will and His Word, and yet most people ignore the Bible. In the Bible, God gives precepts, principles, and promises that can provide guidance in every area of life. Knowing and obeying the Word of God is the surest way to success.

Man cannot control future events. He has neither the wisdom to *see* the future nor the power to *control* the future. For him to boast is sin; it is making himself God (see vv. 13–15). How foolish it is for people to ignore the will of God. It is like going through the dark jungles without a map, or over the stormy seas without a compass.

When we visited Mammoth Cave in Kentucky, I was impressed with the maze of tunnels and the dense darkness when the lights were turned off. When we got to the "Pulpit Rock," the man in charge of the tour gave a five-word sermon from it: "Stay close to your guide." Good counsel indeed!

❀

Applying God's Truth:

1. If you knew you had only one week to live, list all the things you would want to do during that week.

2. What do you think is the difference between *spending* your life doing something and *investing* it in something?

3. Do you have a way of regularly evaluating how productive you are being for God? If not, what can you do to start such an evaluation?

Day 24

Obeying God's Will

Read James 4:15–17

"You ought to say, 'If it is the Lord's will, we will live and do this or that.'"
JAMES 4:15

I t is important to have the right attitude toward the will of God. Some people think God's will is a cold, impersonal machine. God starts it going, and it is up to them to keep it functioning smoothly. If they disobey Him in some way, the machine grinds to a halt, and they are out of God's will for the rest of their lives.

God's will is not a cold, impersonal machine. It is not determined in some mechanical way, like getting a soft drink out of a pop machine. *The will of God is a living relationship between God and the believer.*

I prefer to see the will of God as a warm, growing, living body. If something goes wrong with one organ, the whole body doesn't die: The other parts of the body compensate for it until that organ begins working properly again. There is pain; there is also weakness; but there is not necessarily death.

When you and I get out of God's will, it is not the end of everything. We suffer, to be sure; but when God cannot rule, He overrules. Just as the body compensates for the malfunctioning of one part, so God adjusts things to bring us back into His will.

Applying God's Truth:

1. On a scale of 1 to 10, where 1 is "Do your own thing" and 10 is "Follow God's will exclusively," where would you say you usually are?

2. What are some ways in which you try to determine God's will for your life?

3. What is one decision you are getting ready to make right now for which you first need to seek God's will?

Day 25

Wants and Needs

Read James 5:1–2

> *"Now listen, you rich people, weep and wail because*
> *of the misery that is coming upon you."*
>
> JAMES 5:1

A magazine advertisement told of the shopping spree of an oil-rich sultan. He purchased nineteen Cadillacs, one for each of his nineteen wives, and paid extra to have the cars lengthened. He also bought two Porsches, six Mercedes, a $40,000 speedboat, and a truck for hauling it. Add to the list sixteen refrigerators, $47,000 worth of women's luggage, two Florida grapefruit trees, two reclining chairs, and one slot machine. His total bill was $1,500,000, and he had to pay another $194,500 to have everything delivered. Talk about living in luxury!

All of us are grateful for the good things of life, and we would certainly not want to return to primitive conditions. But we recognize the fact that there is a point of diminishing returns. "Tell me what thou dost need," said the Quaker to his neighbor, "and I will tell thee how to get along without it." The rich men James addressed were feeding themselves on their riches and starving to death. The Greek word pictures cattle being fattened for the slaughter.

Luxury has a way of ruining character. It is a form of self-indulgence. If we match character with wealth, we can produce much good, but if we match self-indulgence with wealth, the result is sin.

Applying God's Truth:

1. Do you have any dreams or fantasies of luxury? If so, what do you sometimes dream about?

2. Do you own anything that you feel you absolutely, positively could not live without? If so, explain why.

3. Do you think you could be extremely wealthy without being selfish or self-indulgent? Why?

Day 26

What Money Can't Buy

Read James 5:3–6

> *"Your gold and silver are corroded. Their corrosion will testify against you and eat your flesh like fire. You have hoarded wealth in the last days."*
>
> JAMES 5:3

It is good to have the things that money can buy, provided we also have the things that money cannot buy. What good is a $500,000 house if there is no home? Or a million-dollar diamond ring if there is no love? James does not condemn riches or rich people; he condemns the wrong use of riches, and rich people who use their wealth as a weapon and not as a tool with which to build.

It is possible to be poor in this world and yet rich in the next world. It is also possible to be rich in this world and poor in the next world. The return of Jesus Christ will make some people poor and others rich, depending on the spiritual condition of their hearts.

A famous preacher, known for his long sermons, was asked to give the annual "charity sermon" for the poor. It was suggested that if he preached too long, the congregation might not give as much as they should.

Yes, money talks. What will it say to each of us at the Last Judgment?

Applying God's Truth:

1. What are some things you have that money can't buy? Do you ever wish you could trade any of those things for cold, hard cash?

2. Would you say you are rich or poor in this world? Will you be rich or poor in the next world?

3. How important would you say money is to you? Why?

Day 27

A Coming Harvest

Read James 5:7–9

> *"See how the farmer waits for the land to yield its valuable crop and how patient he is for the autumn and spring rains. You too, be patient and stand firm, because the Lord's coming is near."*
>
> JAMES 5:7–8

If a man is impatient, then he had better not become a farmer. No crop appears overnight, and no farmer has control over the weather. He must also have patience with the seed and the crop, for it takes time for plants to grow. A Jewish farmer would plow and sow in the autumn months. The "autumn rain" would soften the soil. The "spring rain" would come in February or March and help to mature the harvest. The farmer had to wait many weeks for his seed to produce fruit.

Why did he willingly wait so long? Because the fruit is "valuable." The harvest is worth waiting for. James pictured the Christian as a "spiritual farmer" looking for a spiritual harvest. There are seasons to the spiritual life just as there are seasons to the soil. Sometimes, our hearts become cold and "wintry," and the Lord has to "plow them up" before He can plant the seed. He sends the sunshine and the rains of His goodness to water and nurture the seeds planted, but we must be patient to wait for the harvest (see Gal. 6:9–10).

Here, then, is a secret of endurance when the going gets tough: *God is producing a harvest in our lives.*

Applying God's Truth:

1. What are the situations in which you are usually most impatient? Why?

2. How can a "watchful farmer" mentality help you be more patient during times when your patience tends to wear thin?

3. Why do you think patience is so important as an element of spiritual maturity?

Day 28

Prophet Sharing

Read James 5:10–11

"Brothers, as an example of patience in the face of suffering,
take the prophets who spoke in the name of the Lord."

James 5:10

The prophets encourage us by reminding us that God cares for us when we go through sufferings for His sake. Elijah announced to wicked King Ahab that there would be a drought in the land for three and one-half years, and Elijah himself had to suffer in that drought (see vv. 17–18). But God cared for him, and God gave him victory over the evil priests of Baal (see 1 Kings chaps. 17–18). It has been said, "The will of God will never lead us where the grace of God cannot keep us."

Many of the prophets had to endure great trials and sufferings, not only at the hands of nonbelievers, but at the hands of professed believers. Jeremiah was arrested as a traitor and even thrown into an abandoned well to die. God fed Jeremiah and protected him throughout that terrible siege of Jerusalem, even though at times it looked as though the prophet was going to be killed. Both Ezekiel and Daniel had their share of hardships, but the Lord delivered them. And even those who were not delivered, who died for the faith, received that special reward for those who are true to Him.

The impact of a faithful, godly life carries much power. We need to remind ourselves that our patience in times of suffering is a testimony to others around us.

Applying God's Truth:

1. How many instances from the Old Testament can you think of in which a prophet modeled patience? (If you can't think of several, you may want to do some research.)

2. Have you ever been in the position of a prophet—taking a public and unpopular stand on an issue at the risk of your reputation (or worse)? What happened?

3. When you are in the minority, but know you are right, how do you keep from caving in to popular opinion?

Day 29

Songs and Prayers

Read James 5:13–18

> *"Is any one of you in trouble? He should pray.*
> *Is anyone happy? Let him sing songs of praise."*
>
> JAMES 5:13

Prayer can remove our afflictions, if that is God's will. But prayer can also give us the grace we need to endure troubles and use them to accomplish God's perfect will. God *can transform troubles into triumphs.* Paul prayed that God would change his circumstances, but instead, God gave Paul the grace he needed to turn his weakness into strength (see 2 Cor. 12:7–10). Our Lord prayed in Gethsemane that the cup would be removed, and it was not (see Matt. 26:36–46); yet the Father gave Him the strength He needed to go to the cross and die for our sins.

James indicates that everybody does not go through troubles at the same time. God balances our lives and gives us hours of suffering and days of singing. Mature Christians know how to sing *while they are suffering.* (Anybody can sing after the trouble has passed.)

Praying and singing were important elements in worship in the early church, and they should be important to us. Our singing ought to be an expression of our inner spiritual life.

Applying God's Truth:

1. On a scale of 1 (least) to 10 (most), how would you rate yourself at going to God in prayer during times of trouble? How would you rate yourself at singing His praises when things are going well or not so well?

2. Do you have a song or songs that seem(s) to bring you closer to God? If not, try to choose one today that you can recall during your next stressful situation.

3. In what ways has God recently transformed some of your troubles into triumphs?

Day 30

Winning the Saved

Read James 5:19–20

> *"Remember this: Whoever turns a sinner from the error of his way will save him from death and cover over a multitude of sins."*
>
> JAMES 5:20

What are we to do when we see a fellow believer wandering from the truth? We should pray for him, to be sure, but we must also seek to help him. He needs to be "converted"—turned back onto the right path again.

It is important that we seek to win the lost, but it is also important to win the saved. If a brother has sinned against us, we should talk to him privately and seek to settle the matter. If he listens, then we have "won [our] brother over" (Matt. 18:15).

If we are going to help an erring brother, we must have an attitude of love, for "love covers over a multitude of sins" (1 Peter 4:8). This does not mean that love "sweeps the dirt under the carpet." Where there is love, there must also be truth; and where there is truth, there is honest confession of sin and cleansing from God.

Love not only helps the offender to face his sins and deal with them, but love also assures the offender that those sins, once forgiven, are remembered no more (see Heb. 8:12).

Applying God's Truth:

1. On a scale of 1 (least) to 10 (most), how readily do you tend to confront someone you know who is caught up in some kind of sinful behavior? Why?

2. If you were involved in something sinful and harmful, would you want a friend to lovingly help you get rid of the problem and find your way back to a good standing with God? Why?

3. Do you think it is possible to confront someone about a sin without being judgmental or condescending? How?